Lost In Ohio

Discovering Strange and Historic Places in the Buckeye State

◆ETAOIN PUBLISHING◆
www.etaoinpublishing.com

HURON
PHOTO.COM

Copyright © 2022 by Mike Sonnenberg

All rights reserved. No part of this publication may be reproduced, distributed, or transmitted in any form or by any means, including photocopying, recording, or other electronic or mechanical methods, without the prior written permission of the publisher, except in the case of brief quotations embodied in critical reviews and certain other noncommercial uses permitted by copyright law.

Although the author and publisher have made every effort to ensure that the information in this book was correct at press time, the author and publisher do not assume and hereby disclaim any liability to any party for any loss, damage, or disruption caused by errors or omissions, whether such errors or omissions result from negligence, accident, or any other cause.

Publisher: Etaoin Publishing and Huron Photo LLC
             Saginaw, MI
             www.EtaoinPublishing.com
             www.HuronPhoto.com

Printed in the United States of America

Paperback ISBN 978-1-955474-07-8
Hardcover ISBN 978-1-955474-08-5
Ebook ISBN 978-1-955474-09-2

A Lost In The States Book
www.LostInTheStates.com

Introduction

I have traveled across Ohio many times on the interstate zooming down I-75 and the Ohio Turnpike. If you only view the Buckeye State through your car windows on the Interstate, you are missing out on the history and beauty of Ohio. From the farmland of the northwest to the hills near the Ohio River in the southeast, Ohio has a diverse terrain and a history that goes back to the beginning of the country. After exploring the small towns, historic sites and unique places, I have a new appreciation for the history and people of the Buckeye State. It was an important part in the beginning of the United States, and five presidents came from the 17th state.

The Buckeye State in the heart of the Midwest has some popular tourist destinations including Cedar Point, the Air Force Museum, and Hocking Hills State Park. This book is not about the most popular tourist destinations to visit, although you should visit them if you haven't already. It's about getting off the expressway and finding the little out of the way places that show the character and history of one of the nation's earliest states.

This book is not intended to be a "bucket list" of all the things you should see and do in Ohio, but instead, stories of places, people and things that I found interesting as I traversed the state. Each story in this book is an independent tale about a specific location in the state. You can read them in any order. I do my best to give accurate locations, although some places do not have a specific address, so I give a description of where it can be found. Most places are open to the public and located on public property, but be sure to follow any posted rules and please be respectful of places you visit. Some places are privately owned and are sometimes opened to the public. Although they may not be accessible, they do have an interesting story that I wanted to share, and I hope that you will be considerate of the owners' privacy.

Contents

Chapter 1
Southern Lower Peninsula

Chapter 2
Central Lower Peninsula

Chapter 3
Northern Lower Peninsula

Chapter 4
Upper Peninsula

Chapter 1
Southeastern Ohio

Athens Lunatic Asylum

Location:
100 Ridges Cir.
Athens, OH 45701

Location of cemetery:
172 Water Tower Dr.
Athens, OH 45701

2

The southeastern town of Athens was chosen by the state for a facility to house mentally ill patients of southern Ohio. Built in 1867, the Athens Lunatic Asylum's design and layout was influenced by Dr. Thomas Kirkbride. A prominent physician in the field of mental health, he had published a book on the proper design for mental hospitals. Several buildings around the country followed his concepts and some remain standing today. The massive complex in Athens could provide rooms for 572 patients along with housing for doctors and staff. The hospital also had barns for livestock and land for patients to grow food and garden as part of their therapy. It was not meant to be completely self-sufficient, but it did give patients the ability to work outside and help improve their living conditions.

To outsiders, it looked like an idyllic place to be treated with ornate Victorian style buildings and landscaped grounds for patients to relax. The hospital in the early years was far from what we consider a place of healing. The patients were overcrowded, and the population was more than double the capacity of what was originally designed. The staff also practiced cruel forms of treatments such as lobotomies, water or hydro therapy and electroshock therapy.

3

In the early years of the hospital, many patients were sent to live at the facility for ailments such as alcohol addiction, menopause, and tuberculosis. People suffering from epilepsy were sent to the hospital because the disease was not understood back then and they were thought to be insane or possessed by a demon.

As time passed, the hospital did change the way it treated patients and changed names several times. The hospital closed in 1993; at that time it was called the Athens Mental Health and Development Center, reflecting a more compassionate name than insane asylum. After the facility closed, it was given over to Ohio University and renovated for use as campus buildings. After a naming contest to give the facility a more appealing title, it is now known as The Ridges.

Because of the large numbers of people who died at the asylum, three cemeteries were created on the grounds surrounding the hospital. In the early years, graves were marked by a simple small stone with a number carved into it. By the 1940s, the hospital had begun carving names and dates into the headstones. There are nearly two thousand people buried at the cemeteries and many of them are only known by a number. Some of them were Civil War and World War 1 veterans.

4

The cemeteries sit on the side of a hill near the Water Tower Road that leads to the observatory. Rows of headstones stand on the steep hill with the veterans' graves marked by small American flags. In the woods nearby are a row of old headstones. A nature trail winds its way past them, and they stand as an eerie reminder of past lives at the asylum.

I have visited numerous old cemeteries and had never gotten the creeps, but this one was a little different. Knowing its tragic history and the old worn headstones surrounded by the tall grass while I was there as the sun was setting gave it a spooky feeling. I turned around to see a woman walking out of the woods on the hiking trail. She was not an apparition, but nonetheless, it scared me for a second.

Because of its sad and turbulent history, many believe the buildings and cemeteries are haunted by the spirits of past patients. Tours are given throughout the year of the old asylum, and visitors can learn about its history and paranormal events. You can find more info on the tours at Athenshistory.org

John Wesley Powell Memorial

Location:
202 Main St.
Jackson, OH 45640

Half a block down the street from the courthouse in Jackson is a small building made with stones. They are carved with lettering that declares they were donated from tribes of different states. The front door is lettering that reads Powell Memorial.

Born in 1834, John Wesley Powell came to Jackson, Ohio with his family when he was a young boy. Growing up in southern Ohio fueled his passion for nature and geology.

After studying in Illinois, he joined the Union Army to fight in the Civil War. Rising to the rank of Captain, he commanded Battery F of the 2nd Illinois Light Artillery. His right arm was shot in the Battle of Shiloh and had to be amputated. Despite losing his arm, he returned to battle and continued fighting until the end of the war.

In 1869, he led an expedition covering the entire length of the Colorado River and through the Grand Canyon. The arduous journey lasted for three months and must have been made even more challenging, for Powell with only one arm. After his expeditions exploring the American West, he was appointed the second director of the U.S. Geological Survey in 1881. Two decades later, in 1902, he died and was buried in Arlington National Cemetery.

In 1934, the fraternal order, Improved Order of Red Men, decided to build a monument in Jackson, Ohio. The order is one of the oldest in the United States and descended from the Sons of Liberty. The members were not Native American, but white men who dressed in Indian costumes. It was a strange fraternal order, but like many at the time, men joined for its benefits like life insurance. The order requested that its "tribes" send carved stones for the building of the monument. After three years, and some stones donated by local politicians and businessmen, the monument was constructed. There were challenges in acquiring stones for the monument, and because of this, one of the stones on the rear of the monument was an old tombstone. The monument still stands tucked away in a public square, and I wonder how many people who see it know who John Wesley Power was or his accomplishments.

Lake Powell in Utah and Arizona is named after John Wesley Powell.

Eclipse Company Town

Location:
11350 Jackson Dr.
The Plains, OH 45780

North of Athens, next to the Hockhocking Adena Bikeway, is Johnson Road. Standing alongside it is a row of identical houses and a large two story building. Currently known as the Eclipse Company Town, it was originally known as Hocking. It was built by the Johnson Brothers and the road through town was named in their honor. They started the Johnson Brothers Coal Company that eventually became part of the Hocking Valley Coal Company. The company built the town in 1901 and 1902.

The large two story building was the company store. The mine owners kept track of the amount of coal each worker loaded in the mine. They were given credit at the company store for each ton loaded. Instead of money that they could spend any way they wished, they were forced to use their credit at the company store. As Tennesee Ernie Ford sang, "I owe my soul to the company store", making them slaves to the coal company. The workers with families lived in the company houses and individuals lived in rooms above the company store. Of course, the coal company deducted their rent from the credits they earned in the mine.

The Eclipse Mine Number 4 was next to the town and stayed in operation until it closed during the Great Depression in the

1930s. The mine reopened for a short time during the second World War but closed for good in 1948. The former mine superintendent took ownership of the land and houses. He rented out the houses, and the store was used for various purposes in the following decades, including a machine shop, a barn for storing hay, and a VFW hall.

In 1997, the former town was purchased by a group of five friends with plans on restoring it for future generations. They renamed the area, calling it the Eclipse Company Town in honor of the old mine. The company store was renovated and opened as a restaurant and brewery in 2017. Some of the old houses are used for businesses and others still as private residents. Although it is privately owned, it is an interesting trip through town to see what life was like for miners a century ago.

Nelsonville Brick Park

Location:
620 Lake Hope Dr.
Nelsonville, OH 45764

On a winding road northeast of Nelsonville is a roadside park with some strange looking brick structures. These are the remnants of the old Nelsonville Brick Company. The area around Nelsonville was a popular place for making bricks because of the clay in the ground and the railroad that could haul supplies in and bricks out. The largest brick plant was Nelsonville Brick Company, which started in 1877. At its peak, the plant had one hundred twenty workers. It achieved worldwide recognition after its brick won first prize in the World's Fair in St. Louis.

Through the early 1900s the plant produced large amounts of bricks for roads and buildings. By the 1930s, concrete had become the preferred method of building roads, and the demand for bricks declined. In the 1940s, the plant closed and the structures were abandoned. In the 1980s, a park was created to preserve the remaining structures. The old kilns now stand for people to explore and learn about the history of brick making in Nelsonville.

Nelsonville is also home to the Hocking Valley Scenic Railway. Volunteers give rides on historic trains through the valley.

Shenandoah Crash Site

Location:
N 39° 50.341 W 081° 32.311
On Shenandoah Road west of Ava

Location: Crash Site Number 3
13501 McConnelsville Rd.
Caldwell, OH 43724

The most notable crash of what we would call a "blimp" today would be the crash of the *Hindenburg*. It burst into flames while landing on May 6, 1937. It was one of the earliest disasters to be captured on film as it happened. Most people are unaware of an airship that crashed in southern Ohio about a decade earlier.

Ferdinand Von Zeppelin pioneered the use of rigid airships for Germany at the beginning of the 20th century. The United States Navy began building its own airships inspired by the design of the Zeppelins. The first U.S. airship was built in the hangar at the naval airfield in Lakehurst New Jersey. Construction started in June 1922, and the airship was launched in August 1923. The dirigible was 680 feet long and 78 feet wide, and named the *U.S.S. Shenandoah*. It was the first airship to be lifted with helium instead of hydrogen. Helium gas was scarce at the time, and the largest source was in the petroleum fields in Texas. Most of the nation's supply was used to fill the *Shenandoah's* large gas bags made out of specially treated cow large intestines. If you ever purchased a helium balloon only to have it deflate a few days later, you learn the helium is a small molecule that passes through most materials. At the time, they found that cow intestines could be sewn together with cotton materials to make a bladder that could hold the fine gas molecules.

USS Shenandoah Wreckage National Archives

The ship and its crew flew around the country promoting the navy's ability to build airships. Mooring masts were placed around the country for airships to dock at. The Navy even experimented with mooring masts on the back of naval ships to dock the dirigibles and supply them at sea. Powered by six engines, the *Shenandoah* could reach speeds of 70 miles per hour. On a tragic day, about two years after it was launched, the ship fell out of the sky and crashed in rural southeastern Ohio.

The Navy sent the airship to the midwest on a promotional tour. Comandar Zachary Lansdowne warned of impending bad weather but was ordered to make the flight. The *U.S.S. Shenandoah* encountered a storm on September 5, 1925. It is believed that *Shenandoah* rose too high and the helium bags expanded, breaking apart the rigid air frame. The ship broke into three pieces and plummeted onto the farm fields of Noble County. Fourteen crew members were killed, including Commander Lansdowne. Twenty-nine men clung to the framework of the descending airship and managed to survive the crash.

The devastating incident was never fully investigated. Sightseers and looters descended on the wreckage, and for days after stripped the site of anything they could take. The instrumentation and log books were taken along with personal items of the dead crewmen. There are three sites where the wreckage of the *U.S.S. Shenandoah* came to lay on that fateful day. All of the wreckage is gone now, but a stone monument was placed at site number one as a memorial to the ship and the men who died there.

Commander Zachary Lansdowne was a highly decorated Naval Officer and earned the Navy Cross for his participation in the first transoceanic flight in an airship. He was born in Greenville, Ohio, and his house still stands and is on the national register of historic places.

Moonville Tunnel

Location:
Hope-Moonville Rd.
McArthur, OH 45651

Where Hope-Moonville Rd.
Crosses Racoon Creek
39.30711, -82.32184

The Moonville Tunnel cuts through a steep hill deep in the Zaleski State Forest southwest of Lake Hope State Park. In 1856, Samuel Coe owned the property where the tunnel now stands. He gave the Marietta and Cincinnati (M&C) Railroad permission to run a railroad line across his property. The village of Moonville sprang up near the tunnel. One theory of the name is that a Mr. Moon owned the local general store, and the town was named for it. But it is only a theory because it has never been confirmed in the census that a person by the last name lived in Moonville. The town slowly grew to about one hundred people by the late 1800s. Most of the residents worked in the nearby coal mine. When it closed in the early 1900s, most of the people in Moonville moved away. The last family moved away in the 1940s, and all that remains of the community are the tunnel, cemetery and the foundation of the old schoolhouse.

The tunnel and surrounding area is said to be one of the most haunted places in Ohio. There are several theories and legends as to why. In 1859, local newspapers reported that a brakeman fell from the train as it was passing through the tunnel. When he hit the ground, his leg was crushed by the steel wheels of the train. Another reason for the hauntings is that the town was plagued by an epidemic of smallpox and several people died. Some say the ghost of a railroad worker haunts the tunnel and the light from a lantern he carries can be seen at night.

Since the tunnel was built, four confirmed deaths have occurred in the underground structure. People would hike through the tunnel because it is much easier to walk through the hill than go over it. The tunnel is narrow, and when a train passed through, it would be easy for a hiker to get pulled into the passing train. In later years, before the train tracks were removed, engineers claimed to see many people waving down passing trains on the tracks ahead, and then disappear when they got to their location. This sight was so common that the railroad company issued orders to the engineers not to stop for people in the Moonville Tunnel area.

Getting to the tunnel is an adventure. Miles from any large city, it is a long winding and hilly drive to the secluded area. I recommend driving to it from Route 278 past Lake Hope State Park. My GPS took me in from the south, and the roads were narrow gravel roads that were cut into the side of the hills. If you do not like driving with steep drop offs and no guard trails, I would avoid this route. The old railroad tracks that went through the tunnel are gone, and the former rail line is now the Moonville Rail Trail. Parking can be found on State Road 18 (Hope-Moonville Road) at the Moonville Tunnel Trailhead.

Hope furnace is nearby on Route 278 and is a great place to stop and check out if you are in the area.

Ohio Company Land Office

Location:
On the grounds of
Campus Martius Museum
601 2nd St.
Marietta, OH 45750

In 1786, a group of men in Massachusetts led by Rufus Putnam formed a private land company. The group of prominent men negotiated a deal with the recently formed

United States Congress to purchase about a million and a half acres in the Northwest Territory west of the Allegheny Mountains. After acquiring the land in the Ohio Valley, Rufus Putnam, a former general in the army, led a band of men to create a small settlement near the confluence of the Ohio and Muskingum Rivers. They built a simple log building for an office as they began surveying the land.

To defend against attacks by Native Americans, the men of the Ohio Company built a fortification they named Campus Martius. The name is Latin for "The Fields of Mars". It was the name of a training ground used by ancient Roman Legions. It took a couple of years to build the stockade walls with block houses at each corner. The land office built near the river was moved to the new fortification. Over the years, several buildings were built within the fort, including a brick house for Rufus Putnam.

The fort was built by civilians of the Ohio Company, but run by the military until the Treaty of Greenville was signed in 1795. The treaty ended the fighting between the settlers and

Native Americans. Campus Martius was incorporated into the town of Marietta, named in honor of Queen Marie Antionette and France's support during the Revolutionary War. Most of the original fort is gone, but Rufus Putnam's house and the land office still stand. The log building is the oldest building still standing in the state of Ohio. Campus Martius Museums maintain the buildings and welcome visitors to learn about the early settlement of the Northwest Territory.

Buckeye Furnace

Location:
123 Buckeye Park Rd.
Wellston, OH 45692

In the 1800s, Southeastern Ohio produced much of the nation's iron. The area of the state is known as the Hanging Rock Iron Region and has the natural resources for making iron. The area had approximately sixty-five iron furnaces at its peak, and the stone ruins of their "stacks" can still be seen today. While most are basically rubble, the Buckeye Furnace has been restored to the way it looked when it was producing iron.

In 1851, a group of investors formed the Buckeye Furnace Company and had an iron furnace built by Thomas Price. At its peak of production, the furnace could produce twelve tons of pig iron a day, so named because the iron ingots looked like little piglets when they were being poured in sand next to the furnace. Southeastern Ohio fulfilled the demand for iron during the Industrial Revolution, the Civil War and the expansion of the railroad.

By the late 1800s, other locations and processes had become more economical, and the iron furnaces in the Hanging Rock Iron Region ceased production. The Buckeye Furnace ended the manufacturing of iron in 1894. In 1972, the Ohio Historical Society reconstructed the wood structures around the original stone furnace. It is one of only a handful of old iron furnaces to look the way it did when it was originally built. Visitors can see the old furnace and learn about the process of turning iron ore into pig iron at the Buckeye Furnace State Memorial.

Big Muskie Bucket

Location:
4470 OH-78
McConnelsville, OH 43756

At one time, a giant monster roamed the hilly forests of southeastern Ohio. It was not Bigfoot or any other living creature but a massive mechanical one. It was built in 1967 to strip mine coal from the region. The largest dragline ever built, it was like an enormous crane that had a massive scooping bucket. Named the Big Muskie, it took more than 300 railcars and 250 trucks to haul the components to build it on site. It stood 240 feet tall, and the massive bucket could hold 325 tons of earth in one scoop.

The dragline worked twenty-four hours a day and seven days a week. By the early 1990s, it cost more to operate than the coal it produced, and Big Muskie finally retired. There were efforts to save it for a tourist attraction, but ultimately they failed and it was dismantled for scrap. The only thing that remains, and it is a really large thing, is the bucket it once used. It now stands at a roadside park on Ohio State Route 78 near Jesse Owens State Park. Visitors can climb inside the enormous bucket to see and feel how large it is.

If you like winding and twisty roads, it is a fun trip to the Big Muskie Bucket on Route 78. It is a popular road for motorcycle riders because of all the hills and curves.

Thorla-Mckee Well Park

Location:
18448 Frostyville Rd.
Caldwell, OH 43724

The Drake Well drilled in 1859 in Pennsylvania is considered the first well specifically searching for oil. Long before then, a well that produced oil was sunk in Ohio. Settlers Silas Thorla and Robert McKee noticed that deer were licking a spot on the ground. They believed that it was an underground deposit of salt. The mineral was needed for food preservation and a

30

valuable commodity. In 1814, Thorla and McKee drilled a well and they did find salt, but it was polluted with oil.

They used cotton and wool cloths to soak up the oil and separate it from the salt brine. Wringing the oil from the cloth, they bottled it up and sold it as an elixir to cure an assortment of ailments. A person could claim anything before the Pure Food and Drug Act was signed into law by Theodore Roosevelt.

The well was unstable, and the pressure would sometimes expel salt brine and oil, making it difficult to use. The two men drilled a second well two years later next to the first one using a hollowed out sycamore log as a casing. After drilling to a depth of about two hundred feet, a salt works was set up on the site to process the salt. The well also produced one barrel of oil per week. In 1831, a fire destroyed the salt works, and the endeavor was abandoned.

The well that Thorla and Mckee sunk and the log they used can still be seen surrounded by a metal fence. It is considered America's first oil producing well. The property is now Thorla-McKee Park, and a historical marker recalls the significance of the hole that continues to slowly bubble up salt brine and oil.

> The park is also home to Caboose No. 33. It was built in 1917 and used by the Bellaire, Zanesviile and Cincinnati Railroad.

The Wickerham Inn

Location:
28136 State Rte 41
Peebles, OH 45660

North of Peebles along Ohio State Route 41 stands an old brick building. It is a simple looking two story structure and one of the oldest buildings in southeastern Ohio. It was built in 1800 by Revolutionary War veteran Peter Wickerman. Known as the Wickerman Inn, it welcomed stagecoach riders and drivers traveling along the Zane Trace. The inn was a stop for escaping slaves on the Underground Railroad.

The old inn is also said to be haunted. Legend has it, one night a stagecoach driver stopped at the inn for a night. While drinking a pint of ale, he was bragging about the amount of money and valuables he was carrying. The next morning he never came down from his room upstairs to check out. The innkeeper went up to check on him. He found the room splattered in blood. On the floor near the bed was a blood stain in the shape of a headless body. The driver's body was nowhere in sight, but it is believed he was decapitated based on the blood stain. Since that fateful evening, they say the inn has been haunted by the headless man. Decades later, in the 1920s, when the old inn was renovated, workers found a skeleton under the stone floor of the basement. All the bones were there except for the skull.

The Wickerman Inn is privately owned. If you visit, you can see it from the road, but please be respectful of the owners and do not trespass.

Licking County Historic Jail

Location:
46 S. 3rd St.
Newark, OH 43055

The town of Newark is about forty miles east of Columbus. It has several historic buildings downtown, including the Licking County Courthouse built in 1876. Its stunning architecture has a clock tower that overlooks the city. A few blocks down 3rd Street next to the farmers market is the old historic jail.

The jail was built in 1889, and like many other jails at the time, the sheriff and his family lived at the jail. At the front of the jail, on the first floor, was the living room, dining room and kitchen. On the second floor were the bedrooms. And the third floor was the living area for the matron. She was in charge of the women and children held at the jail. The jail could hold up to 68 inmates with one floor for women and the other three for men.

By the 1970s, the sheriff no longer lived at the jail and the residential space was used for offices. Also in that decade, the women prisoners were moved to another location to have more cells for the men. In the 1980s, a new modern jail was constructed, and the old jail closed in 1987. For years, the old jail was used for storage and housed some of the county's old records. By 2012, interest in the old building had grown. and it was cleaned up and opened to visitors for tours.

Over the decades that it had been in operation, the jail had several deaths within its walls. Inmates committed suicide or died from disease. Three sheriff's had heart attacks while living at the jail. It has some strange and horrific events associated with it. In 1953, fifty-five year old Mae Varner tried to kill herself by overdosing on pain medication. After having her stomach pumped at the hospital, she was held at the jail for physiological observations. She had snuck a match into her cell and set her clothes on fire. The guards beat out the flames, but she died from her burns.

In 1910, Licking County voted to ban liquor, becoming a dry county. The sheriff and other law enforcement officers did not enforce the new ordinance. The Granville mayor deputized many deputy marshals to enforce the law. Seventeen-year-old Carl Etherington was deputized and attempted to serve a warrant at a saloon. He encountered an angry mob, and to protect himself, he shot one of the men who was a former officer in Newark. The mob severely beat Etherington, and he was then arrested and beaten by the police. He was thrown in the Licking County Jail and a mob of about five thousand angry people pulled him out of his cell and hung the deputy marshal on a telephone pole near the jail where he died.

The old jail is considered a hotspot for paranormal activities. It was even featured on an episode of the Travel Channel's *Ghost Adventures*. You can take a tour or hunt for ghosts at the old historic jail. To find out more, visit their website www.lcjail.org.

The Great Coal Mine Fire

Location:
9124 OH-93
New Straitsville, OH 43766
39.586988, -82.224012

Between the towns of New Straitsviille and Shawnee, the ground stays warm all year long, including the middle of winter. This is the result of a coal fire that burns underground which has been burning for more than a century.

The fire started in 1884 during the Hocking Valley Coal Strike. The miners were striking because their wages had been reduced from seventy cents per ton to sixty cents. After the company brought in migrant workers, unknown strikers set coal cars on fire and pushed them into the mine, igniting the underground coal seam. The mine owners tried to extinguish the fire by plugging the entrances and holes, hoping to starve it of oxygen. Their attempt was unsuccessful, and the fire continued to rage underground. At times, flames would shoot one hundred feet into the air from fissures in the ground. The well water used by citizens of New Straitsville came out of the wells steaming hot.

The underground fire became a curiosity, and people came from miles around to see the strange sights. Ripley's Believe It Or Not broadcast a radio report on the "unbelievable" fire. Soon after, locals began charging twenty-five cents for people to see the strange events unfolding underground.

After years of burning, the fire started taking its toll on the town of New Straitsville. Besides workers losing their jobs after the mine closed, the gasses from the fire started seeping into homes, schools and businesses. The coal underground turned to ash and foundations of structures began sinking into the unstable earth.

Starting in the 1930s, the federal government began purchasing the land and incorporating it into the Wayne National Forest. Reclamation efforts have been ongoing to reclaim the land for recreational use, but the fire is still smoldering underground. A historical marker and interpretive site to educate visitors has been erected at the Rock Run Reclamation Site along Ohio State Route 93.

The fire in southeastern Ohio is not the only long-burning coal fire in the United States. The town of Centralia in Pennsylvania is a ghost town after the residents were evacuated because of a coal fire that has been burning since 1962.

Ariel-Foundation Park

Location:
10 Pittsburgh Ave.
Mt Vernon, OH 43050

South of downtown Mount Vernon along the Kokosing River is an eclectic assortment of ruins. Walls from an old building and a smoke stack that serves as an observation tower stand in what is now Ariel Foundation Park. Before it was converted into a park, the site was home to Pittsburgh Plate Glass factory. It was the largest plate glass-making facility in the world and about a million square feet in size.

The plant was constructed in 1902 and employed several workers from the surrounding area. It was left abandoned after it closed in the 1970s. With a large donation for the Ariel Corporation to the Mount Vernon Community Foundation, the site was cleaned up and reclaimed for use as a park. Select portions of the plant remained as part of the park to remind and educate visitors on the park's past.

Modern sculptures and art installments were made using materials from the former glass plant. One notable piece is the river of glass using large pieces that seemingly flow across the landscape. Steel girders from the roof of the building were used in creating a modern sculpture. It was not the first time the girders were salvaged. They originally were used in a building for the 1893 Chicago World's Fair. They were salvaged after the fair and sent to Ohio for use in the construction of the plant.

The most notable structure is the observation tower. It was created by adding a spiral staircase around the old smoke stack that was built in 1951. It is the tallest structure in Knox County, and the newly added 224 steps take visitors to a view that overlooks the area.

The park is officially open from April to November. Some areas are open to pedestrians all year, but if you go, be sure to obey posted signs.

Chapter 2
Southwest Ohio

Lockington Locks

Location:
Intersection of Cross Trail and
Museum Trail Road in Lockington
40.208313, -84.234888

South of Piqua is the small town of Lockington. Here you will find a series of stone structures that look like medieval walls. The name of the town gives a hint as to what they were used for. The Miami and Erie Canal went from Lake Erie in Toledo to the Ohio River near Cincinnati. The two hundred seventy four foot long canal cut through the Ohio countryside and had

46

to traverse several elevations with the highest summit being near Lockington.

The stone structures are what remains of the seven locks used to cross over Loramie Summit. The locks were used to raise and lower boats sixty-seven feet. They consisted of a pair of enormous gates. Boats would be situated between them and then they were closed. The water inside could then be raised or lowered to match the surrounding elevation. It was like a giant water elevator since water does not flow uphill. Construction on the locks began in 1833, and they went into use in 1845 when the Miami and Erie Canal was opened for boat traffic.

It was not much longer after the canal was completed that the railroad began running tracks across Ohio. The railroads diminished the need for canals and a devastating flood in 1913 destroyed part of the canal, putting an end to the waterway. Not much remains of the Miami and Erie Canal today, but the remains of the old locks can still be seen in Lockington.

> The first lock appears to be in better shape than the others because it had some restoration and stabilization work done to it in 2014. The work was done in hope to preserve it for future generations.

47

Frankenstein's Castle
Stone Tower

Location:
Hills and Dales MetroPark,
2655 S. Patterson Blvd,
Kettering, OH 45409
Parking at the Paw Paw Pavillion
39.709704, -84.180444

Hills and Dales MetroPark spans sixty-three acres in the community of Kettering, which is situated south of Dayton. It's a beautiful natural oasis that was created when the founder of National Cash Register Company, John H. Patterson, donated the land to the city in 1907. He hired John Charles

Olmsted and Frederick Law Olmsted Jr. to design hiking trails and landscape the park. The two men were the nephew and son of Frederick Law Olmsted, who designed New York City's Central Park. The park is home to pavilions, ponds and natural settings for visitors to enjoy. But it is a stone tower that stands on a hill in the south end of the park that captures many visitors' attention.

The tower does not have an official name, but it is mostly known as the Witches Castle Stone Tower. It also has other names such as Frankenstein's Castle, Kettering Tower, or simply The Stone Tower. Urban legend has it that the medieval looking structure is haunted and has several wild myths behind the strange hauntings. One such story is that a young woman, learning of her lover's death in the Civil War, climbed to the top of the tower. She jumped off and committed suicide to end her grief. This story is not true because the tower is not that old.

The 56 foot tall tower was constructed in 1940 by the National Youth Administration. It was part of President Franklin Roosevelt's New Deal, and stones from recently demolished buildings were used to construct the tower. For decades, it stood on the hill and visitors could climb it and look out over the park until one tragic day in 1967. Teenager Peggy Ann Harmeson and her boyfriend took shelter in the tower during a storm. The tower was struck by lightning and Peggy was killed, and her boyfriend badly burned. Since that horrific event, the tower has been closed off. I am thinking that is when the rumors of it being cursed began. The tower stands as a reminder to enjoy the surrounding beauty and that life is a fragile thing, and we must enjoy it while we can.

Not far from Hills and Dales Metropark is the Carillon Historical Park, which is home to the Wright Brothers National Museum.

Caesar's Creek Pioneer Village

Location:
3999 Pioneer Village Rd.
Waynesville, OH 45068

Caesar Creek State Park is about forty miles northeast of Cincinnati. It was developed in the 1970s when the Army Corps of Engineers dammed the creek and created a reservoir. It now serves as a lake for the state park and visitors to enjoy.

51

After the completion of the dam, the water would have covered some historic buildings and they would have been lost forever. To save them for future generations, they were moved near an old log cabin. It had been built in 1808 on higher ground and would remain above water. When the state park was being developed, the state turned over maintenance of the cabin and buildings to a local non-profit group. Over the years, several other historical buildings were moved to the site near the old log cabin, and the Caesar's Creek Pioneer Village was born.

The village consists of about twenty buildings. The collection includes a blacksmith shop, school house, broom shed, toll house, carpenter shop, meeting house and several family homes. The grounds are open during the daytime in the summer months. People can wander around the outside of the historic structures and see what life was like a couple of centuries ago. During special events, the buildings are open for visitors to see the interiors. You can find a schedule of events at www.ccpv.us.

The village is a great place to step back in time to see the way people lived before modern conveniences of electricity, indoor plumbing and the internet. Although the village is on state park property, it is not maintained by the state park. A dedicated group of volunteers maintain and restore the buildings in the village.

The original townsite of New Burlington, founded in 1833, was flooded after the construction of the dam. Most of the small farming community was acquired by the federal government to create the reservoir and is now underwater.

Clifton Mill

Location:
75 Water St.
Clifton, OH 45316

In the heart of the Miami Valley is the small town of Clifton. It is mostly known for the historic mill powered by the Little Miami River. Along with the mill, the town has many other old buildings and an interesting history. The river flowing for eons has cut through the earth, making a natural gorge and a perfect location for water powered mills.

Col. Robert Patterson, an ancestor of the founder of National Cash Register in Dayton, John Patterson, chose the Little Miami River for the site of his woolen mill. It furnished material for the American army during the War of 1812. Soon after, five other mills sprang up along the river, including a woolen mill, saw mill, paper mill, barrel mill and a grist mill (used for grinding grains). In 1802, Revolutionary War soldier and frontiersman Owen Davis built the first mill in the Clifton Gorge. The village around the mills became known as Davis Mills. When the village was platted in the 1830s and given a post office, it was named Clifton for the surrounding cliffs in the gorge. The mill that Owen Davis built over two centuries ago is the Clifton Mill that still stands today and is one of the oldest mills in the United States.

Clifton has many historic buildings, including an old blacksmith shop, service station and opera house that is still used by the community for public functions. A wooden covered bridge crosses over the Little Miami River and is used as a pedestrian bridge. It was built in the 1990s to resemble bridges of the past. The Clifton Gorge State Nature Preserve and John Bryan State Park are nearby and offer a chance to experience the natural surroundings of the gorge.

The mill is privately owned and still grinds grain, using water power. Tours are available to see how it operates. It also has a restaurant and gift shop for visitors to get a bite to eat or take home a reminder of their visit. During the Christmas season, the old mill is decorated with four million lights and attracts visitors from far away to see the dazzling display. In 2021, it took third place on the USA Today's list of the ten best holiday displays.

Clifton is the birthplace of Woody Hayes. He was the football coach of The Ohio State University Buckeyes for 28 seasons and won five championships. His father was once superintendent of Clifton Union School.

Johnny Appleseed

Growing up in the midwest, I remember the tall tales of colorful people such as Paul Bunyan, John Henry and Johnny Appleseed. I am not sure if all of them are based on real people, but Johnny Appleseed was the nickname of a real person. Born in Massachusetts in 1774, John Chapman moved to western Pennsylvania when he was a teenager. A few years later, his father and his siblings moved to the Ohio Territory where Chapman worked on his father's farm. He started an apprenticeship at a nearby apple orchard that started him on his journey of growing apple trees.

Chapman traveled around the region, helping people plant and grow apple trees. They were not the apples that most people are familiar with today. They were smaller bitter sour apples used in the making of hard cider. Because of the lack of fresh water, hard cider was safer to drink and was less likely to contain bacteria and diseases. The fact that a person could get drunk from it also helped in its popularity. Having apples to make cider was more of a necessity to survive the harsh conditions of the unsettled midwest. John Chapman was well liked for his kindness and generosity, giving out seeds and helping people plant them. He acquired the nickname of Johnny Appleseed as he traveled around from homestead to homestead.

In the early days of the United States before Ohio became a state, land speculators purchased large tracts of land in the hopes that settlers would be moving to the area. One company, the Ohio Company of Associates, gave away one hundred acres of land to attract settlers. They made deals to people willing to form a permanent homestead. To prove their homestead was permanent, settlers were required to have fifty apple trees. Since it took about ten years for the trees to bear fruit, they could prove that they had lived on the property for more than a decade. Chapman's apple seeds were popular with the homesteaders not only for the apples, but to meet the requirements set forth in their contracts.

Chapman traveled throughout Ohio and the midwest during his lifetime. Around the age of seventy he stayed with a friend in Fort Wayne Indiana. While he was there, he got sick and died in 1845. The exact date of his death and location of his gravesite is not exactly certain, but he was a real person who impacted many lives of early Americans.

The Johnny Appleseed Education Center and Museum is located at 518 College Way, Urbana, Ohio 43078.

Woodland Cemetery

Location:
118 Woodland Ave.
Dayton, OH 45409

The city of Dayton is the home of the Wright Brothers and the Air Force Museum. Visitors to the museum can see hundreds of historic aircraft, including several presidential planes that had the call sign of Air Force One. On a hill in the southeast portion of the city is the Woodland Cemetery and Arboretum. It is one of the nation's oldest garden cemeteries. It is where Orville and Wilbur were buried.

59

Today most people think that visiting a cemetery is kind of creepy, but in the gilded age, cemeteries were designed to be more of a "park-like" setting where the living can spend time with their departed loved ones. The Woodland Cemetery is a beautiful example of a landscaped cemetery with rolling hills and large trees providing shade for visitors. Created in 1841, it is the final resting place for many prominent Ohioans, including writer Erma Bombeck and automotive pioneer Charles F. Kettering.

The grounds are adorned with several beautiful and unique stone markers. One of them is for the grave of Johnny Morehouse. Born in 1855, he was the youngest son of John and Mary Morehouse. His father owned a shoe repair shop in Dayton, and the family lived in an apartment attached to the back of the shop. The shop was near the Miami and Erie Canal, and on August 14th, 1861, young Johnny fell into the canal. His faithful dog tried desperately to pull him out, but the young boy died in the cold water of the canal.

Johnny Moorehouse was buried at Woodland Cemetery. His loyal dog came and laid on his gravesite for several weeks after his death. A special headstone was carved depicting his dog holding him and some of his belongings, including a cap, harmonica, top and a ball. Some say the spirit of a little boy can be seen near the gravesite. I am not sure about that, but visitors moved by his tragic tale leave flowers and little toys at his tombstone.

Also buried at the cemetery are the King and Queen of the Gypsies, Levi and Matilda Stanley. To be clear, the word gypsy is a derogatory word used to describe nomadic people of eastern Europe. Levi Stanley emigrated to the United States in the 1850s, and soon after, many of his family members came to the states, including his mother and father. In their culture, the heads of the family was referred to as king and queen. When the elder Stanleys died, Levi and his wife Matilda became the king and queen of the family.

Levi began purchasing land near Dayton, and his family became well known in the area. When Matilda died in Vicksburg, Mississippi in January 1878, she was embalmed and her body placed in the receiving vault at Woodland Cemetery. It was customary for their family to wait until summer months for burial. Over 20,000 visitors from nomadic families came from across the United States and Canada to pay their respects to the "queen" until she was buried eight months later.

Levi Stanley died while living in Marshall Texas in 1908. He was laid to rest next to his wife, although few people attended his funeral compared to Matilda's.

The cemetery is a beautiful place to visit and an interesting way to learn some of Ohio's history. If you visit, be sure to be respectful and note that it is under security due to vandalism over the years. If you plan on visiting, be sure to check the hours it is open because the gates are closed and access is restricted.

Annie Oakley

Location:
Annie Oakley Park
Martin St.
Greenville, OH 45331
40.099396, -84.629740

Annie Oakley was a world famous sharpshooter who toured with Buffalo Bill's Wild West Show. I had assumed she was born out west and learned her skills with a gun in the high desert, but I was mistaken. She was born Phoebe Ann Moses on August 13, 1860, a few miles north of Greenville Ohio. She lived on a farm with her family, and when she was six years old her father was caught in a blizzard coming back from the mill. By the time he reached the farm, he was frozen to the wagon and near death. His wife and children took him inside to warm up, but the ordeal took a long-lasting toll on his body, and he died a few months later.

Annie learned to shoot a gun when she was eight years old. She quickly mastered the art of shooting and could kill small game. She would take her kill to a nearby store where they would pay her and send it to hotels and restaurants in Cincinnati. Because her family was destitute after her father died, she was sent to live with another family. The family that she called "the wolves" treated her like a slave, and after a few years, she managed to get away from them and lived on her own, and somehow managed to get by.

Traveling marksman and entertainer Frank E. Butler placed a $100 (about $2500 today) bet with a Cincinnati hotel owner that he could outshoot any local marksmen. Butler was surprised to learn his opponent was a five foot tall girl. He lost the bet to Annie after he missed his 25th shot in the competition. Frank became smitten with Annie and courted her for about a year until they married. The couple lived in the Oakley neighborhood of Cincinnati, and it is believed that is where she got her stage name of Annie Oakley.

Traveling all around the world with Buffalo Bill, Annie performed for large crowds and royalty. She championed women's rights and donated much of the money she earned to women's and children's charities. She continued setting shooting records well into her 60s, and in a shooting competition in New York, she shot over one hundred clay pigeons consecutively without missing.

In 1922, Annie and Frank were in an automobile accident in which she was seriously injured. Her health declined for several years later, and the couple moved to Greenville, Ohio, where Annie died at the age of 66 on November 3, 1926. Her body was cremated and her ashes buried at nearby Brock Cemetery. Her husband Frank died eighteen days later, and his body was buried with Annie's ashes.

The National Annie Oakley Center at the Garst Museum in Greenville Ohio displays Annie Oakley artifacts, including guns and gifts given to her by kings, queens and Native American chiefs.

Serpent Mound

A depiction of the serpent mound that appeared in The Century periodical in April 1890, drawn by William Jacob Baer.

Location:
3850 OH-73
Peebles, OH 45660

When I think of ancient civilizations and world heritage sites, I recall places like the pyramids in Egypt or Stonehenge in England, not southern Ohio. But there is a unique and ancient effigy mound in the shape of a snake—the Serpent Mound is about seventy miles east of Cincinnati along the Ohio Brush Creek. It is believed to be thousands of years old. Created by ancient people, it is over 1300 feet long. The head aligns with the summer solstice sunset, and the tail with the winter solstice sunrise. The head of the serpent has an open mouth, and in front of it is a 120 foot long oval. Some scholars believe it represents a snake eating an egg and possibly symbolizes the sun.

In the late 1800s, Harvard archaeologist Fredric Ward Putnum conducted scientific excavations of the Serpent Mound. He determined that it was constructed by early Native Americans using rocks and then covered with a layer of soil. There were no artifacts found inside the Serpent Mound to date exactly when it was constructed or by whom. Two different groups of Native Americans occupied the land surrounding the mound. The Early Woodland Adema culture dated from 500 B.C. to 200 A.D. and the Prehistoric Fort Culture from 1000 to 1650 A.D.

The site has been designated a National Historic Site and is operated by the Ohio History Connection. The site is being considered to be added to the UNESCO World Heritage List. If you want to visit this historic site, be sure to visit Ohiohistory.org for times and dates that the site is open to visitors.

> There are similar serpent effigies in Ontario and Scotland. The word effigy means in the shape of an animal or person.

Cincinnati-Dayton Defense Area

Location:
600 Co. Rd. 37 (Osborn Rd.)
Wilmington, OH 45177

About a mile north of the entrance to Cowen Lake State Park on Osborn Road is a strange looking complex. It has an old rusting guard shack and is surrounded by fencing.

Privately owned and closed off to the public, it was one of many Nike missile sites operated by the U.S. military during the Cold War.

At the end of World War II, a new system was needed to defend against enemy aircraft strikes. With the invention of jet fighter planes, conventional anti aircraft guns were insufficient. Project Nike stationed a series of missiles around the county in case of attack. Four missile sites were placed in the vicinity of Cincinnati and Dayton. Three sites are in Ohio, and one in Indiana. They were located in: Wilmington (CD-27), Felicity (CD-46), Oxford (CD-78) and Dillsboro, Indiana (CD-63).

The sites became operational in the 1960s and remained active until 1970. All four sites were sold off and are now privately owned. Driving down Osborn Road, you can still see the dilapidated complex of buildings from the missile site.

Ulysses S. Grant Childhood Home

Location:
219 E. Grant Ave.
Georgetown, OH 45121

Ulysses S. Grant grew up in a plain looking two and a half story brick house in Georgetown. His father Jesse Grant built the home in 1823, and his family moved into it when he was sixteen months old. Jesse owned and operated a tannery, and the building still stands across the street from the house.

Ulysses spent his childhood in Georgetown and lived in the house until he went to West Point in 1839. The two room schoolhouse he attended is down the street from his boyhood home.

By the 1970s, the old house had deteriorated to the point that it was being considered for demolition. In 1977, Georgetown native and wildlife artist John Ruthven and his wife Judy purchased the house. They restored and furnished the home to the way it would have been in 1839. Opening the home to visitors, it was named a National Historic Landmark in 1982. In 2002, the Ruthvens donated the house to the state of Ohio. In 2013, the house was completely restored for 1.4 million dollars. It remains open for visitors to feel what the 18th president's childhood was like.

The home where Grant was born is in nearby Point Pleasant at the corner of US Route 52 and State Route 232.

John Rankin House

Location:
6152 Rankin Hill Rd.
Ripley, OH 45167

The small town of Ripley sits along the Ohio River at the mouth of the Redoak Creek. The Ohio River Scenic Byway passes through the historic community. In the early 1800s, escaping slaves who were seeking freedom would cross the river into Ohio. Slavery was not legal in Ohio, but federal laws permitted runaway slaves to be captured in northern states and sent back south to their owners.

Ripley resident and Presbyterian minister John Rankin and his wife were early abolitionist and assisted runaway slaves. The Rankins built their modest home in 1825 high up on a hill overlooking the town of Ripley. They lived there with their thirteen children. It is considered one of the earliest "stations" on the underground railroad. With the help of relatives and neighbors, the Rankins assisted hundreds of runways. It is believed that they helped over two thousand escaping slaves to freedom. At times, they had up to twelve runaways living with them. I could not imagine how crowded that house must have been with their children living there too.

While living in Cincinnati, author Harriet Beecher Stowe became friends with John Rankin. The stories she heard from freedom seekers at his home was part of the inspiration for her book *Uncle Tom's Cabin.*

Sorg Mansion

Location:
204 S Main St.
Middletown, OH 45044

Between Dayton and Cincinnati is the town of Middleton. There you will find a massive Richard Romanesque style stone mansion that looks like a castle. Known as the Sorg Mansion, it was built by Paul J. Sorg. He was born in Wheeling, West Virginia in 1840. After serving in the Civil War, he partnered with John Auer, and the two men formed a tobacco company.

Auer was skilled at the process of rolling tobacco, and Sorg, who was skilled at bookkeeping, managed the money.

The two men merged their tobacco company with another one that had ties to Middletown. It was there in 1887 that Paul J. Sorg built his elaborate mansion. It is over thirteen thousand square feet with thirty-five rooms. It has twelve bedrooms and eight bathrooms. Ornate stone carvings adorn the exterior and wood paneling and hand carved trim covers the interior. Paul J, Sorg died in 1902, and the house passed on to his family.

In the 1930s, the home was sold and converted into apartments. After being used as office space and a dance studio, the home was sold to a couple who are in the process of restoring it to its former glory. It is still privately owned but worth looking at from the street and marveling at its exterior.

John Roebling Bridge

View of the bridge in 1907

Location:
Crosses the Ohio River
south of Cincinnati
39.092899, -84.509872

The Brooklyn Bridge was one of the first suspension bridges and an engineering marvel when it was constructed. The man who designed the bridge was John Roebling, and he built a bridge across the Ohio River before the one in New York. The John A. Roebling Suspension Bridge, originally known as the Cincinnati-Covington Bridge, spans the Ohio River between Cincinnati, Ohio, and Covington, Kentucky. With a span of 1057 feet, it was the longest suspension bridge in the world when it opened in 1866.

As commerce increased in Cincinnati and congestion on the river slowed transportation of goods, it became evident that a bridge was needed to cross the Ohio River. There were many challenges to overcome besides spanning the width of the river. One issue was the boat owners did not want a bridge that would impede ship traffic. Another challenge was the politics involved with the states on both sides of the river. Ohio was a free state and across the river, Kentucky was a pro slavery state, and the two could not agree on building a bridge together.

Challenges aside, the Covington and Cincinnati Bridge Company was incorporated in 1846 and they asked John Roebling to design a bridge. It had to be tall enough that steamboats could pass underneath it. Originally, he designed a support in the middle of the river, but that idea was shot down by the riverboat owners, and they demanded the bridge span the river without any obstructions to boat traffic. It took ten years of discussions and compromises to come to an agreement about the design of the bridge, and to find funding from private and government investors.

Construction of the bridge began in 1856. Crews worked on preparing the foundations for the two towers on both sides of the river. Work had to be suspended during the winter months when the river was frozen over. In 1857, work was halted because the Panic of 57 limited the ability to pay for the project, but it was resumed the following year. Work progressed slowly until 1861, and the start of the Civil War stopped all work on the project.

During the war, it was feared that confederate soldiers could attack the city. A floating pontoon style bridge was quickly constructed across the river so Union troops could cross into Cincinnati. After the war, the temporary bridge solidified the need for a permanent bridge. Work resumed on the suspension bridge after funding was obtained by selling bonds. The massive bridge was finally completed and opened to traffic in December 1866. The bridge still remains open to pedestrians and passenger vehicles. Heavy trucks are prohibited in order to extend the life of the historic structure.

The bridge was originally painted brown. In 1976, it was painted blue in honor of the nation's bicentennial.

Mac-O-Chee and Mac-A-Cheek

Mac-O-Chee built by Donn Piatt

Location:
Mac-O-Chee (closed to public)
2319 OH-287
West Liberty, OH 43357

Mac-A-Cheek (open with
admission fee)
10051 Township Rd 47.
West Liberty, OH 43357

79

In the countryside north of Dayton and Columbus is the town of West Liberty. A few miles west of town are a pair of stone castle-like houses with odd names built by two brothers. The castles are named Mac-O-Chee and Mac-A-Cheek. The names are derived from the Mekoche, a division of the Shawnee people.

The two homes were constructed by brothers Donn and Abram S. Piatt in the 1860s. Their father Benjamin Piatt purchased 1700 acres of land in 1817 for a farm that he called Mac-O-Cheek where the two brothers were raised.

Donn Piatt started his career as a lawyer but went on to

Mac-A-Cheek built by Abram S. Piatt

become a successful journalist after serving as a Union officer during the civil war. He began building his home Mac-O-Chee in 1864 and completed it in 1871. His brother Abram farmed and served as a general in the Union army during the Civil War. He began building his home Mac-A-Cheek at the same time as his brother in 1864 and finished in 1879. The two houses are about three quarters of a mile from each other. They are both made using stone quarried nearby and have ornately carved woodwork.

After Abram's death in 1912, his son William McCoy Piatt inherited the house. He had a large collection of artifacts and built a cabinet to display them. People would visit his home to see the curiosities he had on display in the cabinet. From that point on, the home has been opened to tourists to see the home and artifacts.

The homes were passed on through generations of the Piatt family until 2019. The family decided to sell Mac-O-Chee. It was becoming difficult to maintain both homes so they sold Donn's home and used the money to maintain Mac-A-Cheek. The historic home is still used for weddings, receptions and other events. The new owners of Mac-O-Chee are in the process of restoring it.

Please note that both homes are privately owned, but Mac-A-Cheek is open at times to the public for tours.

Governor Bebb's Cabin

Location:
Governor Bebb MetroPark
1979 Bebb Park Ln.
Okeana, OH 45053

Near the Indiana border northwest of Cincinnati is the Governor Bebb Metropark. Within the park boundaries is an old log cabin where William Bebb was born in 1802. He was raised in this cabin; his family was one of the earliest white settlers in the area. In his 20s, he became a school teacher at the local school, and after marrying his wife, the two opened a boarding school on their farm.

While teaching, Bebb studied law and took the bar exam in 1831. After passing it, he began practicing law in nearby Hamilton. While there, he became active in politics, and in 1840, he stumped the state for Harrison and Tyler. In 1846, he was nominated for governor by the Whig party, and after winning the election, he served as the state's nineteenth governor. He only served one term, but his term was extended a few months until the discrepancies in the election of 1848 could be sorted out.

After serving as governor, he moved to Washington D.C. and worked in the pension office for President Abraham Lincoln. Following his time in Washington, he moved to a farm in Illinois, where he died in 1873.

Besides the Bebb cabin, the park is home to a few other historic buildings and an 1850s covered bridge that was moved to the park in the 1970s. Admission to the park is $8 per vehicle.

Chapter 3
Northeast Ohio

Zoar Village

Location:
198 Main St.
Zoar, OH 44697

If you were traveling down Ohio State Route 212 south of Bolivar in a Delorean with a flux capacitor, you would think you traveled through time. The historic Zoar Village has many of its original buildings and houses that have stood for almost two centuries. Most have been restored to the way they looked when they were originally constructed.

Zoar was settled in 1817 by German religious dissenters who emigrated from southeastern Germany to escape persecution for their religious beliefs. They thought that the church should be simple and bereft of all ceremonies and emphasized a mystical and direct relationship with God. They did not celebrate baptisms, confirmations or other religious holidays.

In 1819, they organized a communal society called the Society of Separatists of Zoar and purchased five thousand acres of land with a loan that would be due in 1830. Without means to pay for it, they were blessed when the state of Ohio decided to run the Ohio and Erie Canal through a portion of their property. The state gave the Zoarites the option of digging a portion of the canal. With the money they earned, they were able to pay off the loan and have some left over.

The group lived in peace and prosperity for a few decades but eventually voted to disband in 1898, and divided the property up among the remaining members. Because the village lasted for nearly eighty years, it was one of the most successful communal towns in the United States. Today the village is a

National Historic Landmark overseen by the Zoar Community Association. Many of the homes and businesses are privately owned but welcome tourists to step back in time. Visitors can see the Zoar Gardens along with shops, museums and restaurants and spend a day in a simpler time.

> Not far away from Zoar is the Fort Laurens Museum showcasing the location of Ohio's only Revolutionary War fort.

Death of Pretty Boy Floyd

Location:
Beaver Creek State Park
Co. Hwy. 428
East Liverpool, OH 43920
40.714112, -80.588292

Beaver Creek State Park sits near East Liverpool, Ohio not far from the border of Pennsylvania. The park stretches out along the Little Beaver Creek River and has some historic canal locks and buildings for visitors to learn the history of the area. At the southern end of the park is a historic marker that marks the death of Charles Arthur Floyd. He is most commonly known by his nickname Pretty Boy Floyd. He got the name when he worked in the oil fields around Kansas City, Missouri. He would wear a white button up dress shirt and black slacks to work, and his fellow co-workers gave him the nickname, which he despised.

Working in the oil fields during the Great Depression did not earn enough income for Floyd, and he turned to robbing banks to raise his income. He was suspected of committing about a dozen murders, most of them being police officers. After the death of John Dillinger, Pretty Boy Floyd was named as Public Enemy No. 1 by J. Edgar Hoover.

On his way with his partner Adam Richetti from Youngstown, Ohio to his home in Oklahoma, their car broke down near Wellsville Ohio, and the two men caught the attention of local law enforcement. The police captured Richetti, but Floyd managed to escape. The FBI and local police quickly went on a manhunt for the notorious criminal.

Floyd stopped at the farm of Mrs. Ellen Conkle where he asked for something to eat and a ride to Youngstown. It was there that law enforcement officers spotted him, and he tried to escape by running through the nearby cornfield. Before he could make it into the cover of the tall corn plants, he was shot twice and fell to the ground, and died about fifteen minutes later on October 22, 1934. The farmhouse is gone, but a historical marker now stands near the spot where the infamous criminal took his last breath.

Floyd's body was taken to a mortician in East Liverpool and embalmed to be sent back to his home in Oklahoma for burial. The mortician made a death mask of his face which is now at the East Liverpool Police Museum. A copy of the death mask can be seen at the historic Spread Eagle Tavern in Hanoverton, Ohio.

Lanterman's Mill

Location:
Mill Creek Metropark
Parking at E. Park Drive
Youngstown, OH 44511
41.067702, -80.683639

Mill Creek flows north into the Mahoning River in Youngstown Ohio. The creek cascades down a rocky ledge to create a beautiful waterfall. Next to the falls is the historic Lanterman's Mill. It is an impressive structure built in 1845 by German Lanterman and his brother-in-law Samuel Kimberly.

The mill was originally powered by a large wheel but converted to a turbine for water to pass through. It processed grain from local farms using three different grinding stones. By the 1890s, roller mills were a more economical means of grinding grain, and the Lanterman Mill shut down its operations.

In 1891, Youngstown attorney Volney Rogers purchased large tracts of land along Mill Creek. After acquiring land from more than ninety land owners, Rogers had the land declared as a park by the state legislature. The Mill Creek Park was officially opened in 1893. The old mill was used as a facility for the new park. It had a bathhouse, concession stand and a ballroom. During the winter months, it was used for storage. In the 1930s, the first floor was converted into a nature museum. Visitors could look at the many mounted birds and animals on display along with other exhibits.

In the 1980s, the mill was restored back to its original use as a grain mill. The interior beams were repaired or replaced, and the exterior was given a facelift and new windows. The original equipment was gone, but new grinding stones and replica machinery was constructed and installed. A new observation deck was added to the outside for visitors to view the creek and falls. The building is now operating as it did over a century ago and is a gem in Mill Creek Metropark. If you visit, the parking lot for the mill can be found off E. Park Drive a few hundred yards north of State Route 62.

The park is also home to other historic structures, including the Mill Creek Furnace, suspension bridge, log cabin and the Hopewell Furnace.

Austin Log Cabin

Location:
3798 S Raccoon Rd.
Canfield, OH 44406

South of Austintown on South Racoon Road is an old log cabin. For decades, it was hidden from view. Now, you are probably wondering how a large log cabin next to a busy road could be hidden. It was covered up by modern building materials and siding. In 1973, St Andrew's Episcopal Church purchased what they thought was an old abandoned house.

94

During the process of demolition, log beams were discovered, and it was determined that this was no ordinary abandoned house.

Volunteers carefully removed the modern brick and siding from the house, revealing the hand hewn log house. The "steeple" style joints in the corners proved that the house was built prior to 1824. When the historical society did some research, they found out the house was constructed by John Packard. He purchased land from Calvin Austin who worked for the Connecticut Land Company. Austintown and the township was named for him.

The log house changed hands a few times through some of John Packard's ten children and then through several other owners. In time, they added some other buildings, including a hog barn and chicken coop. They also modernized the home with new siding and some additions until it no longer looked like a log cabin. After raising funds by the community, the cabin was restored to the way it was when it was first constructed, and then artifacts and furniture from the period were added. The house now serves as a reminder of the area's humble beginnings and a museum which is open on the first Sunday of every month.

Molly Stark Park

Location:
7900 Columbus Rd. NE.
Louisville, OH 44641

North east of Canton is a county park. It is unlike most county parks because in the middle is a large abandoned building surrounded by a chain link fence. It was built in 1929 as a tuberculosis hospital. The Molly Stark Sanatorium was built as a place for patients to recover in a beautiful and natural setting. The Spanish revival design had open verandas, passageways and balconies for people suffering from tuberculosis to benefit from the fresh air.

The disease attacks the lungs, and in the 1800s, it was sometimes called consumption because it caused the patient to lose weight and destroyed the body and organs from within. There were few options for treatment at the turn of the century other than providing fresh air and a clean place to live. Patients at the sanatorium were moved to the fourth floor, and as their symptoms improved they were moved down a floor. When their health improved enough, they were moved to the first floor where they could wander the grounds and gardens.

By the 1950s, antibiotics had dramatically reduced the number of people suffering from tuberculosis and the building's name changed to the Molly Stark Hospital. The building continued treating patients, but over time the facility became outdated. In 1995, the hospital closed because it was not cost effective to renovate the old building. A few investment companies looked at converting the building to a nursing home or retail space. but the cost of dealing with the asbestos was cost prohibitive. In 2009, the county's parks board of commissioners purchased the property for one dollar. With a two hundred thousand dollar grant, the grounds were cleaned up and a fence installed around the building, and the Molly Stark Park was created. People are welcome to walk the grounds and marvel at the old architecture through the fence. The building is closed to visitors and tours, but hopefully one day a use can be found for this historic structure.

Molly Stark was the wife of Revolutionary War hero General John Stark, known for the famous quote "live free or die". During the war, Molly turned her home into a makeshift hospital and nursed her husband's troops during a smallpox epidemic and attended to the wounded.

Pvt. William J. Knight Monument

Location:
53 E. Main St.
Apple Creek, OH 44606

A team of renegade soldiers sneaking two hundred miles behind enemy lines and stealing a vehicle to escape back and destroying everything behind them sounds like a modern day action movie. It actually happened during the Civil War, and the vehicle was a steam locomotive. A band of 22 Union

99

soldiers and two civilians were led by secret agent James Andrews to Marietta, Georgia. There they hijacked a steam locomotive named "The General". They uncoupled the passenger cars and absconded with the engine and three freight cars.

The key person in the plan was Apple Creek, Ohio native William J. Knight. Before the war, he was an engineer for the Atlantic and Western Railroad. His expertise was needed to drive the train. Andrew's Raiders drove the train from Atlanta, Georgia to Chattanooga, Tennessee, destroying tracks, bridges and telegram wires along the way.

Unfortunately, the men never made it back to Union Territory. They abandoned the locomotive to escape, but were captured by the Confederate Army. Andrews and seven other men were hanged, and eight soldiers were exchanged for Confederate prisoners in the north. Eight soldiers, including Knight, escaped from a Confederate Prison and made their way back to Union territory.

Knight and seventeen others were awarded the Medal of Honor for the raid. The story of the raid captured the attention of the public, and Knight traveled the country, telling stories of his role in the daring mission. William J. Knight died in Stryker, Ohio in 1916, at the age of seventy nine. He was laid to rest in Oakwood Cemetery near Stryker. His hometown of Apple Creek erected a memorial to the brave engineer who ran the locomotive during Andrew's Raid.

It was common during the time to have large panoramic panels painted depicting scenes of a story during a speaking engagement. Before projectors and power point, these paintings helped tell a story. One of the panorama panels used by Knight is on display at the Ohio History Center on 17th Avenue in Columbus.

Mohican Memorial Shrine

Location:
1000 OH-97
Perrysville, OH 44864

Mohican State Forest is located between Columbus and Cleveland, and has over 4500 acres of wilderness to explore. State Route 97 passes through the area, and here you will find a stone shrine erected to honor the Ohioans who died fighting for freedom.

The Mohican Memorial Shrine was built in 1947 by funds raised by more than sixty thousand Women's Clubs members from across the state. They required that all materials and companies involved in the construction of the shrine be native to Ohio. The sandstone blocks to construct the walls were quarried nearby. The timber for the roof came from trees grown in the surrounding forest. Roof tiles were manufactured in New Lexington and floor tiles in Zanesville. An art glass studio in Columbus created the stained glass windows that adorn the walls of the shrine. They depict scenes of buckeye trees and cardinals, which is Ohio's state bird.

A book with over twenty thousand handwritten names sits on an altar under glass. It lists the names of all the Ohioans who were killed in World War II, the Korean War, the Vietnam War, the Persian Gulf War, and the Afghanistan and Iraq operations.

A set of eight binders are located in the center of the room and duplicate the book's listings by county and by war for the convenience of visitors seeking names. Women's Clubs help maintain the shrine and keep its roll of honored dead updated.

Ohio State Reformatory

Location:
100 Reformatory Rd.
Mansfield, OH 44905

The town of Mansfield sits between Columbus and Cleveland and is the home of a massive castle-like structure. It was not home to royalty but rather to people who broke the rules. The massive stone structure was the Ohio State Reformatory and is famous for being the location for filming of The Shawshank Redemption.

Construction began in 1886 and was named the Intermediate Penitentiary. Its main purpose was to reform young men who were too old for juvenile prison but were first time non-violent criminals. The inmates were given eighteen months to reform their behavior and after a review could be released for good behavior. If they did not meet the requirements for release, they had to remain for another eighteen months and try again.

Because of budget constraints, the prison was not fully constructed until 1910. Its imposing stone walls and styling was meant to intimidate and inspire prisoners to change their behavior. The six-tier high east cell block remains the largest free standing steel cell block in the world.

In the 1960s, the prison was converted into a maximum security facility. It was never intended for such a purpose, and with its age and deterioration, the conditions of the old prison began to suffer dramatically by the time it had been standing for a century in the 1980s. Because of the deplorable conditions, inmates sued the state of Ohio, and a judge ruled the prison had to be shut down. It closed in 1990. The historic prison sat empty for years until a local non profit group purchased it for one dollar. They raised funds to stabilize the old prison and now offer tours to visitors. You can find out more at their website. www.mrps.org.

Besides being a popular location for movies and TV shows, it is a popular location for ghost hunters. Over 200 people died at the prison, including two guards during an attempted escape, and many believe their spirits are trapped in the old stone walls and steel cells.

Punderson Manor Lodge

Location:
Punderson State Park
11755 Kinsman Rd.
Newbury Township, OH 44065

About twenty miles east of Cleveland is Punderson State Park. Like many of Ohio's state parks, it offers camping, hiking and a chance to enjoy nature. Like other state parks, it also has a lodge for guests to spend a night or two, but unlike the other parks, Penderson's lodge has a unique history and is said to be haunted.

In 1806, Lemuel Punderson moved from Connecticut and settled in what is now Newbury, Ohio. Exploring the area and finding what he called "the big pond", he built a cabin next to it for workers to construct a mill and distillery. After construction of the mill was finished, Lemuel and his family moved into the cabin. He operated the mill until he died of malaria in 1822. The name of the pond was changed to Punderson Pond in his memory.

In 1902, W.B. Cleveland, son of Moses Cleveland, who founded the city that bears his name, purchased most of the land surrounding Puderson Pond. He built a large home for his wife and family. He used the property for a dog kennel where he raised prize winning bird dogs. Cleveland became ill in 1920 and was no longer able to use or maintain the property. The property was then leased to Karl Long, a builder in Detroit.

An agreement was made that Long could make minor changes to Cleveland's former home. In 1925, Long tore down everything except the two chimneys and built the current Tudor style mansion that stands today. The Great Depression devastated Karl Long's finances, and he defaulted on his payments to Cleveland. The property was then used as a girls summer camp, but eventually it was sold to the state of Ohio in 1948. The state renovated the lodge in 1965, adding twenty-four rooms and twenty-six cottages. Punderson State Park and Lodge officially opened in 1966.

It became evident that something strange was happening in the lodge. Guests would call down to the lobby and complain about the noise coming from the room next door when no one was staying in it. One guest even complained about the party in the room upstairs when they were staying in a room on the top floor. Employees have reported witnessing strange events: faucets being turned on and off by themselves and pencils flying across the room. If you are looking to stay overnight in a beautiful old historic mansion and you love ghost stories, then Punderson Manor is a place you should visit.

Squire's Castle

Location:
2844 River Rd.
Willoughby Hills, OH 44094

What looks like a medieval stone castle stands in the North Chagrin Reservation, which is part of the Cleveland Metropark. It was built as a gatehouse for a mansion that was never constructed. I can only imagine how large and opulent the mansion would have been considering how ornate the gate house was.

Feargus B. Squire was an executive with the Standard Oil Company and former mayor of Wickliffe, Ohio. Around 1890, he purchased about five hundred acres of land east of Cleveland. He planned to build a large English style country estate, and in 1895 he had this stone gatehouse constructed. Taking three years to build, the walls were quarried from local sandstone, and the building originally had three floors.

Having difficulty in finding labor for the remote location at the time, Squire gave up building a mansion on the site. He used the gatehouse as a cottage, but his wife did not like staying there. The gatehouse-turned-cottage did not have electricity, natural gas, running water, or sewer. I can see why his wife, being accustomed to the modern conveniences of Cleveland, did not enjoy living in the cottage.

Squire rarely used the cottage, and he sold it and the property to developers in 1922. Shortly afterwards, the developers went bankrupt and the Cleveland Park Board purchased the property in 1925. The old gate house was vandalized over the years, and the structure was renovated in 1995. The upper floors were removed and the basement filled in. It was not what it used to be, but at least a portion of it was saved for park visitors to enjoy.

A false legend has it that Squire's wife fell down the stairs and died in the old gatehouse. They say her spirit haunts the structure, but that is not true because she died at their family home in Wickliffe, Ohio in 1927.

The Legend of Gore Orphanage

Location:
Gore Orphanage Rd.
Amherst, OH 44001
41.355315, -82.335111

While doing research, I come across many tragic and strange urban legends. Some are wild fictional tales, and others are true stories about horrific events. The legend of Gore Orphanage is a wild tale based on a series of events. The legend goes that Gore Orphanage along the Vermillion River burned down, killing several children. Remains of the building can be seen in the woods and the spirits of the children roam the area.

To start with, there was no such place as Gore Orphanage. A road of that name does exist. It was originally named Gore Road. Not for blood and horror, but for the shape of a piece of cloth used in making a woman's skirt. There was an orphanage on the road and that was probably when the name changed. The name of the orphanage was Light of Hope. It was a farm that was established by Reverend Johann Sprunger and his wife. They built it after their first orphanage in Berne, Indiana burned down but no one was killed or injured in the fire.

The new orphanage in northern Ohio in 1902 housed about one hundred twenty children. A few years later, some of the children ran away and told of the horrific conditions and abuse. They were forced to live in rat infested barracks and fed very little food. Treated like slaves, they were forced to work on the farm, and many of them were whipped by Sprunger. He would also rent out children to other farmers in the area. When they were investigated in 1909, the Sprungers admitted to the abuse, but they were not prosecuted because there were no laws prohibiting it in Ohio at the time. Johann Sprunger died two years after the investigation, and the orphanage was officially shut down.

During that same time period, one of the most horrific events in Ohio and the United States occurred in the town of Collingwood east of Cleveland. In 1908, a fire started in a three story elementary school. One hundred seventy six students were burned or trampled to death when they were trapped in the fire. The children tried to exit down the front stairs but were blocked by the flames. Trying to escape out the rear of the school, the doors opened inward, and many of the students were crushed up against the doors, desperately trying to open them.

At the southern edge of the Orphanage's farmland was an old abandoned mansion. Named Rosedale, the massive Greek revival house was built in 1841 by Joseph Smith. He moved to the area from Massachusetts and had great success as a farmer. He built the home for his family, and after losing a fortune in railroad investments, he had to sell the house in the 1870s.

The Swift Mansion before demolition from the Library of Congress National Archives.

Spiritualist Nicholas Wilbur purchased the home and moved in with his family. It was said that he would hold seances with his wife and children to speak with the dead. At that time, spiritualism was all the rage, and it was not uncommon for people to try to communicate with spirits. The Wilburs moved out of the house, and by 1901, it was abandoned. Four of their grandchildren died of diphtheria after they moved away, but rumors persisted that they were buried on the property.

While the house sat abandoned in the early 1900s, local teenagers dared each other to enter the home, saying that it was haunted. Vandals set fire to the mansion, and it burned to the ground in 1923. In the trees off Gore Orphanage Road are some stones used in the foundations of the old mansion. The tragic events in the region, an old abandoned mansion, and a road named Gore Orphanage have combined to become the urban legend of the Gore Orphanage. I am not sure who owns the property of the former mansion or if it is open to the public.

Some people have claimed to hear the sounds of children crying in the woods surrounding the old mansion's stones. One theory is that it's the sound of trucks on the 80/90 Turnpike passing over the nearby Vermillion River Bridge.

Marblehead Lighthouse

Location:
110 Lighthouse Dr.
Marblehead, OH 43440

The Great Lakes currently has over two hundred lighthouses standing on the shores of its five lakes guiding ships and sailors around the inland waterway. The oldest lighthouse still standing on the Great Lakes is on Lake Erie in Ohio. The Marblehead Lighthouse stands at the tip of Marblehead Point and marks the entrance of Sandusky Bay. It was constructed in 1821 from limestone quarried nearby. The base of the fifty-foot tall tower is twenty-five feet in diameter, and the walls are five feet thick. The first keeper was Revolutionary War veteran Benjah Walcot. He lived in the keeper's house built near the tower and tended the light every night. After his death in 1832, his wife Rachel took over the responsibility of lighting the lamps and maintaining the lighthouse.

Over the two centuries, the lighthouse has had every form of illumination. It started out with thirteen lamps using whale oil. It was converted to kerosene, and its burning flame shone through a rotating fresnel lens. It was then changed to an electric lamp and finally to a modern LED light. The lighthouse was automated in 1958, and a keeper was no longer needed at the historic lighthouse. The Ohio Department of Natural Resources took over maintaining the lighthouse, and a state park was created on the land surrounding the beacon. The old keeper's house is now a museum.

Next to the lighthouse is a former life saving station. It was built in 1876 with Lucien Clemons as its first commander. A year before, he and his two brothers saved two sailors after their ship wrecked off the peninsula.

The Franklin Castle

Location:
4308 Franklin Blvd.
Cleveland, OH 44113

Near downtown Cleveland is what some people consider the most haunted house in Ohio. I am not sure if there is any way to confirm that, but it was featured on an episode of the Travel Channel's Ghost Adventures.

In 1881, German immigrant, and Cleveland banker, Hannes Tiedemann, built the large four-story stone home on Franklin Boulevard. The area was one of the most prestigious in the city, and Tiedemann's house stood out among the surrounding homes. Shortly after moving into the home, Hannes' fifteen year old daughter died from Diabetes. Soon afterwards, his mother-in-law died, and over the next three years, three more of his children died.

To distract his wife from the death of their children, Tiedemann began adding new construction to their home. He added a ballroom which runs the length of the house on the fourth floor. Workman also added turrets and gargoyles to the exterior, making it look more like a castle. In 1895, his wife

Louise died from a liver disease, and with her death, Hannes' entire family had died. The next year, Tiedemann sold the house, and he died in 1908 with no relatives to inherit his wealth.

From 1921 to 1968, the house functioned as a home to various German and cultural organizations. It is rumored that it was used as a speakeasy by bootleggers during prohibition. In 1968, a family with six children purchased the house and while living in it claimed to have encounters with spirits in the home. They sold it soon afterwards, and the new owner gave ghost tours trying to raise money to convert it into a church. During this time, the notoriety of the house being haunted grew. How true the hauntings were, I am not sure, but I am sure stories were exaggerated to sell more ghost tours.

In early 1984, Michael DeVinko, Judy Garland's fifth and last husband, purchased Franklin Castle. He spent over a million dollars making renovations to the house. He even tracked down some of the original furnishings for the house. He sold the castle in 1994, and since then, various people have owned it over the years. The house on Franklin Street is still privately owned. Although it is not open to the public, you can get a good view of it from the street and wonder about the man who built it and the death of his family.

Garfield's Houses

Location:
Birthplace Replica Log cabin
4350 Som Center Rd.
Moreland Hills, OH 44022

Fairlawn Home
8095 Mentor Ave.
Mentor, OH 44060

In the trees next to the Moreland Hills Police Department is a log cabin. It is a replica of the cabin that James A. Garfield, the nation's 20th president, was born in. The original location of the cabin is about a quarter mile away near the Chagrin River. The future president was born on November 19, 1831, and was the youngest of five children. His father Abram Garfield came to the area as a worker to dig the Ohio and Erie Canal. He died when James was two years old, leaving him to be raised by his mother Eliza.

Poor and fatherless, James was mocked by other children. He spent his time reading to escape his difficult life. When he was seventeen, he left home and looked for work at the port in Cleveland. Being rejected there, he found work leading a team of mules towing canal boats. About six months later he became ill and moved back home. After his health improved, he went off to Geauga Seminary, starting his path to becoming a lawyer and politician.

In 1876, Garfield's success in politics led him to purchase a farm near Mentor, Ohio, about thirteen miles away from the rustic cabin where he grew up. Over the next few years he built additions onto the home, making it a marvelous place for his wife and family. His mother came to live with them; it was a big change from the little log cabin where they lived when James was a young boy.

During the 1880 presidential campaign, Garfield gave speeches to the press from the front porch of his home. They camped out on the lawn and gave it the name "Lawnfield". After winning the election, James A. Garfield would only be president for a short time. He was shot at a Washington train station about four months after taking office. He was struck by two bullets, one in the arm and the other in the back. Badly injured, it was not the bullet that killed him. He was slowly healing, but the doctors, with their unsterilized hands and instruments poking around looking for the bullet, caused the wound to get infected. He died on September 19, 1881, about two months after he was shot. He was laid to rest in Lake View Cemetery in Cleveland and a large stone memorial was erected for the assassinated 20th President of the United States.

James Garfield was the last president to be born in a log cabin. The replica of his cabin is open for tours on select days. His "Lawnfield" home is a National Historic Site run by the National Park Service.

Chapter 4
Northwestern Ohio

Bellefontaine's Landmarks

Location:
Oldest Concrete Street
101 E. Court Ave.
Bellefontaine, OH 43311

Highest Point in Ohio
2280 OH-540.
Bellefontaine, OH 43311
40.370295, -83.720204

The town of Bellefontaine northwest of Columbus has two notable landmarks. One is man made and the other is natural. Campbell Hill is located about a mile outside of downtown and is the highest point in Ohio. It was named for Charles D.

Campbell who owned the land from 1896 to 1937. In 1951, during the Cold War, the military established the 664th Aircraft Control and Warning (AC&W) Squadron on the hill as part of the North American Air Defense Command (NORAD). It was part of an elaborate radar system that scanned the skies looking for enemy aircraft and missiles. The military closed the site in 1969, and it was converted into a civilian trade school in 1974. In a section off the parking lot is a marker for the highest point in Ohio where visitors can sign a guest book.

The other notable landmark can be found next to the Logan County Courthouse in downtown Bellefontaine. East Court Avenue is the world's oldest concrete street and was paved in 1891.

George Bartholomew came to the area because it had the necessary raw material to manufacture concrete. The dirt roads of the day were rough and dusty, and during rain storms, they turned to mud. Bartholomew convinced the city council to try a sample section on Main Street to see how well the concrete could hold up to traffic. After a successful test, Bartholomew was permitted to pave the streets surrounding the courthouse. Because the use of concrete had never been done before, they required Bartholomew to put up a five thousand dollar bond for five years to repair or remove the streets if they degraded quickly. The bond was unnecessary as Court Avenue remains today. The other streets needed to be replaced because of water and sewer repairs, but Court Avenue, although it has some repairs, is still open to traffic.

Bellefontaine also claims to be the home of America's shortest street. McKinley Street, named for the President, is only fifteen feet long.

Bloody Bridge

Location:
Junction OH-66 and Co. Hwy.-182
St. Marys, OH 45885
40.617787, -84.352699

Near Spencerville on State Route 66 is an old steel truss bridge. It crosses what was once the Miami Erie Canal and has been given the gruesome moniker "Bloody Bridge". Legend has it that a horrific murder took place on the bridge or previous bridge that splattered it in blood.

131

As the story goes, it took place during the heyday of the canal in 1854. Two men, Bill Jones and Jack Billings, were smitten for Minnie Warren. Both were mule drivers who pulled the boats along the canal. There were two men and only one woman, so one of them was going to be the loser. Minnie fell for Jack, and Bill's heart was broken.

Returning from a party, Minnie and Jack were surprised on the bridge by Bill, who was carrying an ax. He swung the impromptu weapon, decapitating Jack and spilling his blood on the bridge. Terrorized by what just happened, Minnie screamed and fell off the bridge, and drowned in the canal.

After the murder, Bill disappeared, probably ashamed by what he had just done. A few years later, a skeleton was found in a nearby well. Some people believed it was Bill's, and he committed suicide by jumping into the well. Others thought maybe he had been thrown into the well in a bit of vigilante justice. Exactly how true the story is remains up for debate, but there is a stone marker near the bridge that was erected in the 1970s that recalls the legend of the bloody bridge.

Established in 1924, Ohio State Route 66 runs north and south from Piqua to Fayette. It is not to be confused with Route 66 that runs from Chicago to L.A.

Fort Amanda

Location:
22800 OH-198
Lima, OH 45806
40.680670, -84.26/808

Auglaize River flows north through western Ohio up to the Maumee River and into Toledo. In the early days of the United States, before the railroad and automobile, the river was a primary means of transportation. During the War of 1812,

133

General William Henry Harrison ordered that a fort be constructed along the Auglaize River by Lt. Col. Robert Pogue. He had his soldiers build a simple wooden fort with stockade walls and blockhouses on the corners. He named it Fort Amanda after his twelve-year-old daughter.

Fort Amanda became an important staging point on the Auglaize River. Troops and supplies stopped at the fort and boarded boats to travel up the river to Fort Meigs in present day Perrysburg. Opposite the river from the fort, a boatworks was set up to build flat bottom boats using local trees for timber.

After the war ended, the military abandoned the fort, and by 1817 local settlers began using parts of it for shelter and housing. Over time, everything related to Fort Amanda was gone. In 1913, the land where the fort once stood was sold to the state for one dollar. Two years later, a fifty foot stone obelisk was constructed to mark the site where the fort once stood.

The area also includes a cemetery and park for visitors to explore. It is a great way to learn a little history while hiking the nature trails.

Lima Locomotive Works

Location:
Lincoln Park
1139 E Elm St.
Lima, OH 45804

Lincoln Park can be found in the town of Lima, and there you will find an old steam locomotive, caboose, and Pullman car on display. The locomotive is historically significant to the town of Lima and rests in a fitting place after years of traveling the rails. Known as the Nickel Plate #779, it was the last steam locomotive made at the Lima Locomotive Works. The Nickel Plate Road was the nickname given to the NYC&STL Railroad Company that ran a rail line from New York City to Chicago then on to St. Louis.

The Lima Locomotive Works started in 1878 after James Alley contracted the Lima Machine Works to build a steam locomotive that Ephraim Shay had designed. Shay's unique design used side-mounted steam pistons that turned a horizontal shaft to drive the wheels. It was like four wheel drive for locomotives. The compact design that provided excellent traction and pulling power was popular with lumber companies for hauling timber out of difficult terrain. The sales of the Shay locomotive enabled the company to expand into building larger steam locomotives.

Lima's mechanical engineer William E. Woodard developed a new efficient way for the locomotive to utilize steam which he dubbed "Super Power". It made for a more powerful locomotive and continued the company's success. The Lima Locomotive Works built over seven thousand steam locomotives before it finally ended production in 1949, when it built the locomotive on display in Lincoln Park. It continued on for a few more years building diesel locomotives, but they were not as successful as other companies and they closed in the 1950s.

The most famous locomotive built in Lima was the 1225 for the Pere Marquette Railroad. It was the inspiration for *The Polar Express* written by Chris Van Allsburg. It has been restored by the Michigan Steam Railroading Institute and operates out of Owosso, Michigan.

Brumback Library

Location:
215 W Main St.
Van Wert, OH 45891

In the town of Van Wert is a unique looking building. It serves as the Brumback Library, and the fact that it looks like a castle and is filled with books makes it a castle of knowledge.

138

The most interesting feature of the library is not its architecture, but its history. It was the first county library in the United States.

In 1890, twelve women in Van Wert formed the Van Wert Ladies Library Association to establish a subscription library for residents in the area. A few years later, a city tax funded the library, making it free to all residents. Local businessman John Brumback donated money to construct a new library building. Before construction began, John Brumback died, and his family oversaw the completion of the new library. They wanted it to be a library for the citizens of Van Wert County.

With support of local farmers and before a tax could be levied county wide, the Ohio legislature had to pass a new law allowing for the new tax. It was the first time such a law or library was created in the United States, making it the first county library system in the United States. The building was constructed in 1899. It has had an addition added to it and has been modernized with the latest technology but still retains its castle-like appearance and holds an important place in history.

Fort McArthur Cemetery

Location:
Approx. 10750 Co. Rd. 115
Kenton, OH 43326
40.663601, -83.673841

In a farmfield northwest of Kenton is a small military cemetery with sixteen tombstones. They mark the final resting place of soldiers stationed at Fort McArthur. Shortly before the start of the War of 1812, American General William Hull needed troops to fight the British in the Detroit area of Michigan. As soldiers marched north, they crossed the Scioto River. To protect the soldiers from the pro-British Native Americans, a fort was constructed by Col. Duncan McArthur.

During the war, up to one thousand men were living at the fort. Not only did they face threats from the British and Native Americans, but also the diseases carried by the mosquitoes in the surrounding swamps. The fort is long gone, but the headstones and cemetery remain. Sadly, the tombstones are marked "unknown" and do not bear the names of the men who gave their lives in support of the newly formed United States of America. A historical marker stands next to the road reminding people of Fort McArthur. A path about one thousand feet long leads to the small military cemetery. Depending upon which crops are growing at the time, the little cemetery may be hidden from view from the road.

> Col. Duncan McArthur went on to become the eleventh governor of Ohio.

Merchant Ball

Location:
Marion Cemetery
620 Delaware Ave.
Marion, OH 43302
In the Northeast
section of Cemetery
40.577767, -83.120119

The historic cemetery in Marion covers over one hundred fifty acres and has numerous headstones and monuments. One monument in particular has intrigued people ever since it was placed in the cemetery over a century ago. Charles B. Merchant was a prominent resident and businessman in Marion. When

142

he died in 1896, his family placed a large monument at his gravesite to honor his memory.

A large black granite ball was placed on a stone plinth. The ball was polished smooth except for a small circular section. When the five thousand pound ball was placed on the mount, the rough section was facing down so that it would not be seen. A few years later, someone noticed that the rough spot was now facing outward. Somehow, the sphere had rotated. The massive ball was lifted and the spot rotated back down, and this time some tar was added to the stone base to keep the sphere from moving.

Once again the ball rotated, despite the addition of the adhesive tar. To this day, the ball continues to rotate over time. Visitors to the cemetery can see the circular spot on the sphere that was once facing down. No one knows why or how the ball is moving. Some speculate that it may be supernatural forces.

A similar memorial known as "The Witch's Ball" can be found at a cemetery in Memphis Michigan. It also rotates and was featured on *Ripley's Believe It or Not*. Some scientists have speculated that the freeze and thawing cycles in the spring and fall have caused it to move.

Black Beetle

Location:
Amtrak Station
Paige Street and N. Lynn Street
Bryan, OH 43506

The town of Bryan is located in the northwest corner of Ohio. It has a small train depot that still operates as an Amtrak station. In the parking lot is a historical marker that recalls the fastest train in America. The sixty-seven miles of railroad track from Toledo, Ohio to Butler, Indiana is the longest multiple track straight railroad line in the world. It was on this stretch of track that the New York Central Railroad Company tested the feasibility of operating high-speed passenger service.

In 1966, the New York Central Railroad modified a passenger rail car. They added an aerodynamic cowling around the bottom and on the top two jet engines for power. The engines were second-hand General Electric J47-19 jet engines, originally used as boosters for the Convair B-36 Peacemaker intercontinental bomber. The railcar M-497 was nicknamed the Black Beetle by the press and tested on July 23, 1966. The railcar with the jet engines strapped to the roof reached a maximum speed of 183.68 mph, an American rail speed record that still stands today.

Hopley Monument

Location:
1517 E Mansfield St.
Bucyrus, OH 44820
(Across From Burger King)

In Bucyrus, an old stone monument stands under the trees of a golf course along the old Lincoln Highway. The highway was the first automobile road that traversed the country from New York City to San Francisco, California. John E. Hopley served as the first Ohio state consul to the Lincoln Highway for fourteen years.

When he died in 1927, this monument was erected in his memory. It was made using stone collected from places that were tied to his life. Some stones came from his birthplace, Elkton, Kentucky. Others came from countries where he served as United States Consul at Southampton, England, appointed by President William McKinley and promoted to consul of Montevideo, Uruguay, by President Theodore Roosevelt. One stone was from Lincoln's birthplace since the highway was named after him. The old highway was replaced by the turnpike that crosses northern Ohio, but motorists can still drive the old highway.

A section in Ohio that ran through Marion, Kenton, and Lima was bypassed by a straighter route to the north. Upset, the citizens of those towns claimed the southern route as the Harding Highway, after hometown President Warren Harding.

The Dungeon in Northern Ohio

Location:
622 Croghan St.
Fremont, OH 43420

In downtown Fremont behind the Sandusky County
Courthouse is an old sandstone building. From the front, it
looks like a Victorian-Romanesque style house. From the side,
an additional three story wing comes off the rear and has bars
on the window. They are there because the old structure at one
time served as the county jail and sheriff's residence. When it

was dedicated in 1890, the keynote speaker was former United States President Rutherford B. Hayes, who was a resident of Fremont. President Hayes was an advocate for prison reform, and at the time the jail was built, it was a modern facility with cells designed with prisoner safety in mind. What lies underneath the building was far from safe and humane for early prisoners of Sandusky County.

In the 1840s, during the beginning of Sandusky County, log cabins with iron bars on the windows were used to confine people who broke the law. The primitive building did not serve its intended purpose well because it had dirt floors and a few prisoners dug down under the wall and escaped. After a few years, it was evident that some other form of incarceration was needed. Instead of building up, they went down and dug a dungeon lined with stone walls. The prisoners were held in dank cells poorly illuminated by kerosene lamps. The Dungeon was used for over a decade until a new jail was built on top of it.

The old jail finally closed in the 1990s after a new jail, to meet current standards, was constructed. There was talk about razing the old building, but it was decided to use it as office space for the county. Over the years, people have noticed strange things happening in the old building. They have heard strange sounds and footsteps of people who were not there. In the middle of the night, the motion detectors will go off when nothing is on the video surveillance.

I can't say for sure if the old jail is haunted, but there were some tragic events that took place within its walls. One inmate in the old dungeon who had been arrested for murder had a visitor slip him a razorblade. He used it to commit suicide in his cell. On the third floor is an old gallows that was used to hang prisoners sentenced to death. The last hanging was done in 1883. John W. Radford was hanged for shooting and killing his wife.

The Sandusky County Convention & Visitors Bureau gives tours of the historic jail. They also host special events and ghost hunts throughout the year. You can visit their website at www.sanduskycounty.org/jail to learn more.

The Mill and the Lock

Location:
Ludwig mill providence metropark
13265 S. River Rd. (County Rd. 53)
Grand Rapids, OH 43522

Providence Park sits along the Maumee River southwest of Toledo. Not only is it a beautiful and peaceful setting with tall trees shading a path along the river, but it is like stepping back in time. It is the only working historic lock on the former Miami and Erie Canal. During the weekends visitors can ride a replica of a canal boat that is towed by a team of mules. Long

151

before electric vehicles, airplanes and trains, the towboats were a popular means of transportation through Ohio. Riders can experience the sensation of being raised or lowered on the old historic lock next to the Isaac Ludwig Mill.

In the 1830s, Peter Manor worked out a land grant with Chief Tondoganie of the Ottawa Indians. He established the town of Providence and set up a sawmill along the river. Shortly afterwards, the state of Ohio required him to surrender his sawmill under eminent domain to make way for the canal. Manor worked out a deal giving him perpetual water rights for a new mill along the canal. In 1847, he contracted Pennsylvania boat builder Isaac Ludwig to construct a new mill. Manor died before the mill was completed, and Ludwig purchased the property and finished construction of the mill.

Ludwig operated the mill for almost four decades before retiring. He sold the mill to Augustine Pilliod. In 1895, Pilliod modernized the mill with new water turbines and a steam engine. In 1908, he added a generator to the steam engine, providing electricity to the local community. According to historians, every evening at 8:55, the generator was slowed down, dimming the lights to remind residents that the electricity would be cut off at 9:00pm when the steam engine was turned off for the night.

In 1971, Isaac Ludwig's grandson Cleo Ludwig, who owned the L-K Restaurant chain, purchased the historic mill and donated it along with Peter Manor's water rights to the Toledo Area Metroparks. The mill and lock was restored to the way they would have been in the early 1900s. On the weekends, the mill grinds grain as the canal boat is towed past, reminding visitors of days gone by.

The L-K Motel and Restaurant chain were popular from the 1940s until they ended in 1989. At their peak they had over 150 locations. The first location started by Cleo Ludwig and Robert Kibbey was in Marion, Ohio.

Killing Spree Ends

Location:
Intersection of
US-224 and OH-637
40.931727, -84.475852

Driving down the roads through the farmland in northwestern Ohio, I came upon a historical marker with the title **Killing Spree Ends Here** in 1948. It stands at the intersection of Stemen Road and U.S. 224, and is a reminder of the evil that people can do and the bravery of the people who stop them.

Robert M. Daniels and John C. West became friends while doing time at the Ohio Reformatory in Mansfield. On July 9, 1948, after they were paroled, the two men, in their twenties, shot and killed a Columbus bar owner during a robbery. The two then decided to exact revenge on some of the guards at the prison where they were incarcerated. On July 21, 1948, they looked for the home of "Red" Phillips, and when they could not find it, they instead went to the home of John Niebel, the head of the prison farm. They took him, along with his wife and 21-year-old daughter, to a cornfield and executed them.

The next day, James Smith and his wife were driving to get ice cream when Daniels and West forced them off the road. They shot and killed Smith as his wife ran away. They stole their car and headed towards Indiana. Truck driver Orville Taylor had stopped at a rest area with four brand new Studebakers he was hauling to West Virginia. One of the men shot Taylor, and Daniels climbed into one of the cars. West hopped into the cab of the truck and drove away.

To capture the men, police set up roadblocks across northwestern Ohio. A roadblock on US Route 224 was manned by Van Wert County Sheriff Roy Shaffer, Frank Friemoth, the county game warden, and Sergeant Leonard Conn of the Van Wert city police. When the car hauler driven by West stopped at the roadblock, Sheriff Shaffer climbed up and looked in the cars, where he saw Daniels hiding in one of them. Soon after, West jumped out of the truck, shooting at the other two law enforcement officers and hitting both of them. As Sergeant Conn fell to the ground, he shot West, striking him in the head between the eyes. West died shortly after, and Daniels was taken into custody. The two officers recovered from their gunshot wounds. Six months later, Robert Murl Daniels was executed on Jan. 3, 1949.

Fossil Park

Location:
5705 Centennial Road
Sylvania, OH 43560

Northwest of Toledo near the Michigan border in the town of
Sylvania is one of the most unique parks in the country. Fossil
Park allows visitors to search through dirt and shale piles to
find fossils. Material from a nearby quarry is dumped in the

park. Tools are not allowed to be brought into the park, but work benches, brushes and water for cleaning rocks and fossils are available.

The fossils are not of dinosaurs, but plants and small sea creatures from millions of years ago. Back then, northwest Ohio was a great sea teeming with life. Brachiopods, coral, and more than two hundred species of prehistoric life were trapped in the rocks for fossil hunters to find.

The park was created in 2001 as part of the Olander Park System. If you are a young kid, or an old one, digging around in the unique park is a fun experience, and hopefully you can find a fossil to take home as a souvenir. The park is completely free and has bathrooms and a bike trail.

> I recommend doing a little research on searching for fossils before you go. There are some signs to inform visitors, but I wish I had learned a little more before I went.

The Battle Of Fallen Timbers

Location:
Falling Timbers Battlefield
4949 N. Jerome Rd.
Maumee, OH 4353/

Fallen Timbers Monument
5798 State Park Rd.
Maumee, OH 43537

Motorists zip through the 475 and US 24 interchange near Perrysburg southwest of Toledo. Signs for Fallen Timbers Battlefield stand along the expressway, but I wonder how many people know about the importance of the historic battle.

The Treaty of Paris ended the Revolutionary War in 1783. British forces still remained in the Northwest Territory, the land northwest of the Ohio River. They allied with the Native American tribes to resist the expansion of the United States. Two American military expeditions into the Northwest Territory by generals Josiah Harmar and Arthur St. Clair in 1790 and 1791 ended in failure.

President George Washington ordered General "Mad" Anthony Wayne to end the unrest in the territory. Wayne acquired the nickname "Mad Anthony" for his bold and successful storming of a British fort at the Battle of Stony Point, New York, in 1779.

On August 20, 1794, Wayne led American troops to victory in a battle with a confederation of Native Americans whose leaders included Chief Little Turtle (Miami), Chief Blue Jacket (Shawnee) and Chief Buckongahelas (Lenape). The battle took place near the Maumee River where a tornado had passed through and toppled over the trees in the area.

A year after the decisive battle, the Treaty of Greenville was signed in present-day Greenville, Ohio. The Indians ceded land to the Americans in the Great Lakes Region, including much of present-day Ohio, which, in 1803, became America's 17th state. The battlefield has become a National Historic Site. The battle remains an important part of American history because it proved that the new country was willing to fight for expansion to the west.

The site consists of two locations. One is at the battlefield that includes a visitors center. And the other, about a half mile away, is a monument that has a statue of General Wayne with a Native American and a frontiersman.

Tri State Marker and
the Toledo War

Location:
Ohio, Michigan, and Indiana
Tri-State Border
41.69645758011927,
-84.80595941372101

The northern border of Ohio cuts into Michigan where the states meet up with Indiana. Near the tri-state intersection is a boulder that reads: 130 feet south is the point where Indiana, Michigan, and Ohio meet. This marker was erected by the Hillsdale County Historical Society—1977.

Michigan ended up with an odd notch because Ohio, which had already become a state in 1803, refused to relinquish Toledo to Michigan. The Northwest Ordinance of 1787 established an east-west line drawn from the southern tip of Lake Michigan across the base of the peninsula. A line was drawn across a map that intersected Lake Erie north of the Maumee River. When Michigan applied for statehood in 1833, its surveyors found the line intersected Lake Erie about eight miles south of the Maumee River. The land in contention became known as the Toledo Strip.

Both Michigan and Ohio claimed ownership of the Toledo Strip. Politicians from Ohio protested Michigan's application for statehood and claimed that Toledo was theirs, knowing that it was an important port on the Great Lakes. This led to some serious altercations, including the time the Michigan Militia captured nine surveyors and arrested some Ohio officials. The feud became known as the Toledo War, and although no one was hurt or injured in the so-called "war", it showed how ingrained in their position each side was. In a compromise, Washington D.C. decided to give Toledo to Ohio and the Upper Peninsula to Michigan, which is why the border of Ohio angles up above Toledo.

Indiana officially became a state in 1816, about twenty years before Michigan. When Indiana surveyed their northern boundary, instead of starting at the southernmost tip of Lake Michigan, they started about ten miles north in order to include several miles of Lake Michigan shoreline. In the early 1800s, it was important to have access to the Great Lakes since shipping was the primary means of transportation and commerce in the region. Indiana's survey is the other reason why Michigan ended up with a notch at the southern border.

There is not a lot to see at the Tri-State point except farmland, trees and the stone marker, but it is one of those places that you can say you have visited.

Ending

I enjoyed my time traveling around Ohio. Through big cities and small towns, exploring the hills and forests of Southern Ohio and the farmland in the northwest. I noticed several banners mounted on utility poles. Each one proudly displayed a photo of a different veteran who served in the military. It was a reminder of the sacrifices many people have made for me to pursue my happiness. I am fortunate to be able to travel around this wonderful country and enjoy the freedom that so many brave men and women have fought for. Thank you to all the veterans who continue to defend the United States of America.

I hope you enjoyed reading this book and are inspired to get lost in Ohio.

I hope you will continue
to follow my journey at

www.lostinthestates.com

Made in the USA
Monee, IL
06 October 2022

15373644R00098